Traditional Crafts from the
CARIBBEAN

Traditional Crafts from the
CARIBBEAN

by Florence Temko

with illustrations by Randall Gooch

Lerner Publications Company • Minneapolis

To Rachel, Perri, David, Dennis, Janet,
Tyler, and Yolanda, again.

Over the years, I have tucked away bits of information in my files that have contributed to my fascination with crafts. They were gathered mainly from personal meetings, books, magazines, libraries, and museums in the United States and abroad. I regret it is no longer possible to disentangle these many and varied resources, but I would like to acknowledge gratefully and humbly everyone who has helped to make this book possible. Thanks also to Professor Robert Brictson, a collector of arts and crafts, who offered me the benefit of his experience of living in the Caribbean.
—Florence Temko

The publisher thanks John Nunley of the St. Louis Art Museum, St. Louis, Missouri, for his help in preparing this book.

Lerner Publications Company
A division of Lerner Publishing Group
241 First Avenue North
Minneapolis, MN 55401 U.S.A.

Website address: www.lernerbooks.com

Temko, Florence.
    Traditional crafts from the Caribbean / by Florence Temko ; with illustrations by Randall Gooch.
        p.   cm. — (Culture crafts)
    Includes bibliographical references and index.
    Summary: Provides instructions on how to make traditional Caribbean Island handicrafts such as Jamaican woven fish, Puerto Rican vejigante masks, and tap-tap trucks.
    ISBN 0-8225-2937-8 (lib. bdg. : alk. paper)
    1. Handicraft—West Indies—Juvenile literature. [1. Handicraft—West Indies.]
I. Gooch, Randall, ill. II. Title. III. Series.
TT32 .T46 2001
745'.09729—dc21   00-008968

Manufactured in the United States of America
1 2 3 4 5 6 – JR – 06 05 04 03 02 01

CONTENTS

WHAT ARE CRAFTS?

All over the world, people need baskets, bowls, and clothes. In modern times, people make many of these things in factories. But long ago, people made what they needed by hand. They formed clay and metal pots for cooking. They wove cloth to wear. They made baskets to carry food. We call these things "crafts" when they are made by hand.

Grandparents and parents taught children how to make crafts. While they worked, the elders told stories. These stories told of their family's culture—all of the ideas and customs that a group of people believe in and practice. Children learned these stories as they learned the ways of making crafts. They painted or carved symbols from those stories on their crafts.

6

Year after year, methods and symbols were passed from parents to children. Still, each bowl or basket they made would look a little different. A craft made by hand—even by the same person—never turns out the exact same way twice.

People who are very good at making crafts are called artisans. Many artisans still use the old methods. They make useful things for themselves and their homes. Some artisans also sell their crafts to earn money.

Left to right: A painted tile from Turkey, a Pueblo Indian pitcher, a pot from Peru, and a porcelain dish from China

MATERIALS AND SUPPLIES

Some of the suggested materials for the crafts in this book are the same as those used by Caribbean artisans. Others will give you almost the same results. Most materials can be found at home or purchased at local stores. Check your telephone book for stores in your area that sell art materials, craft supplies, and teachers' supplies. Whenever you can, try to use recyclable materials—and remember to reuse or recycle the scraps from your projects.

MEASUREMENTS

Sizes are given in inches. If you prefer to use the metric system, you can use the conversion chart on page 58. Because fractions can be hard to work with, round all metric measurements to the nearest whole number.

FINISHES

The crafts in this book that are made from paper will last longer if you brush or sponge them with a thin coat of finish. These are some choices:

White glue (Elmer's or another brand) is the most widely available. Use it at full strength or dilute it with a few drops of water. Apply it with a brush or small sponge. (The sponge should be thrown away after you use it.) White glue dries clear.

Acrylic medium is sold in art supply stores. It handles much like white glue. You can choose a glossy (shiny) finish or a matte (dull) finish.

CARIBBEAN CRAFTS

The Caribbean (kair-uh-BEE-uhn *or* kuh-RIH-bee-uhn) Islands stretch between North and South America, separating the Atlantic Ocean on the east from the Caribbean Sea on the west. The four biggest islands are Puerto Rico (PWAIR-toh REE-koh), Cuba (KYOO-buh), Jamaica (juh-MAY-kuh), and Hispaniola (hiss-pan-YOH-luh), which the countries of Haiti (HAY-tee) and the Dominican Republic (doh-MIN-uh-kuhn ree-PUHB-lik) share. The terrain of most of the islands ranges from sandy beaches to rugged mountains. Plants thrive in the tropical climate, providing materials for weaving. The sea offers coral and shells for jewelry.

The first inhabitants of the Caribbean Islands were Taino (TYE-noh), Carib (KAH-rihb), and Arawak (ar-uh-WAHK) Indians. The Carib people coiled ropes of wet clay into pots. Arawaks often added animal or human heads made of clay to their pots. They made hammocks and baskets from plant materials.

In the 1400s, Europeans arrived in the Caribbean—first the Spanish, and later the Dutch, French, and English. The Europeans brought Christian religious art and many new crafting materials, such as glass beads and yarn, to the islands.

Europeans enslaved Africans and brought them to the Caribbean. African people had a long tradition of metalworking. They also continued to carve masks and other items of wood and to decorate the crafts as they had in their homeland.

All three cultures—Indian, European, and African—have influenced Caribbean arts and crafts. Caribbean artisans rely on materials found locally. They are very inventive in using and recycling any available materials into practical things. Families make most crafts for home use, but they often sell extras at local open-air markets for cash income.

Contemporary island artisans aim to preserve old craft techniques in their new designs. The governments of some of the islands encourage the creation of crafts by establishing centers where local work is displayed and sold.

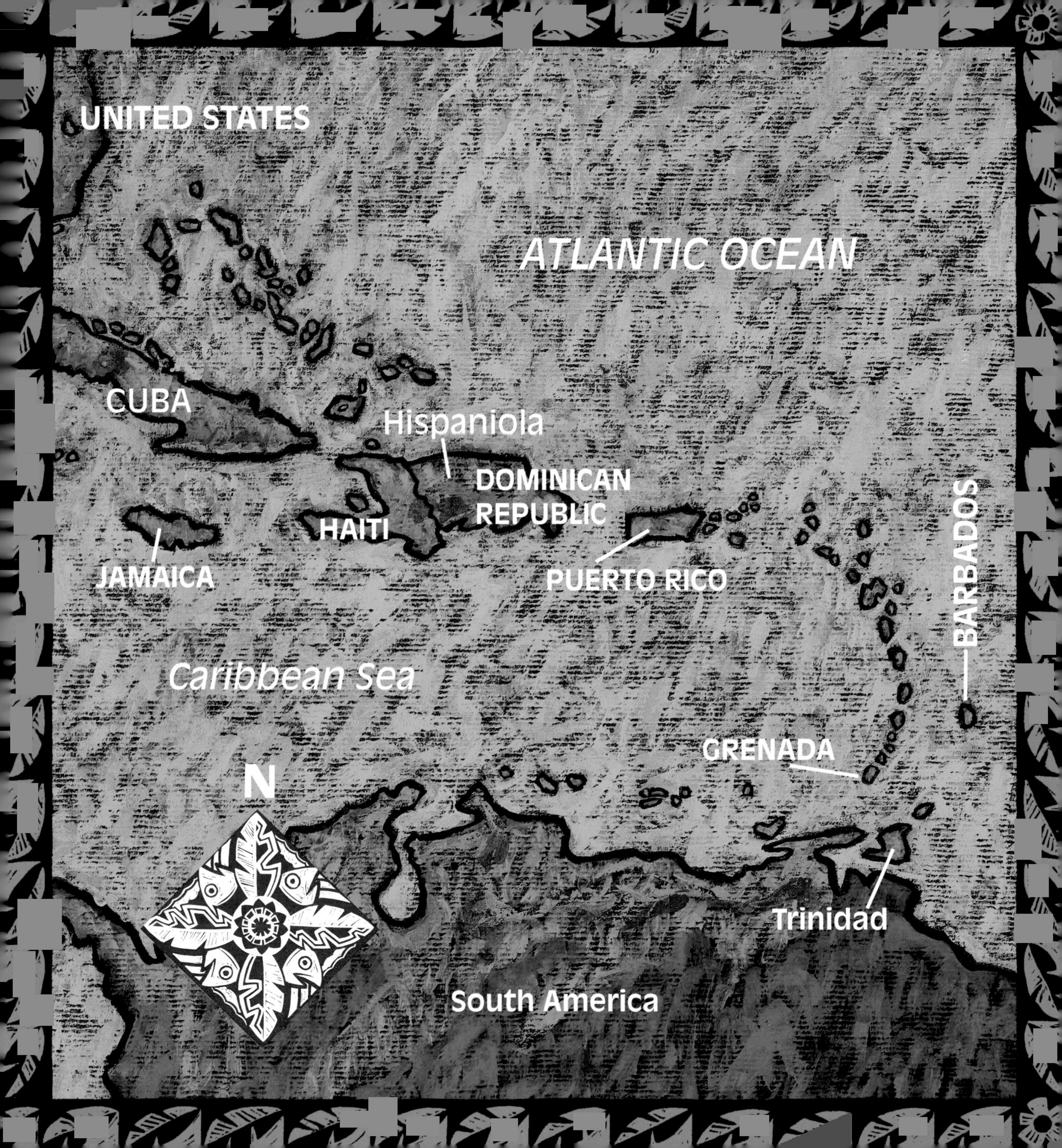

UNITED STATES

ATLANTIC OCEAN

CUBA

Hispaniola

DOMINICAN
REPUBLIC

HAITI

JAMAICA

PUERTO RICO

BARBADOS

Caribbean Sea

GRENADA

N

Trinidad

South America

Barbadian Shell Crafts

A small box decorated with shells can make a great gift.

SHELL DECORATION

The people of Barbados (bahr-BAY-dohs) can find seashells of many sizes, shapes, and colors on their beaches. They craft the shells into necklaces or glue them in decorative patterns onto furniture, boxes, plaques, and other things. In the 1800s, Barbados was often the last stop before home for sailing ships returning to New England from overseas

Barbados is the easternmost of the Caribbean Islands. The flat, rocky island has less natural vegetation than other islands in the area, but shells are a plentiful crafting material.

voyages. Many sailors bought shell-crafted items as gifts for their families. Wooden frames covered with colored shells were, and still are, very popular. The shells are arranged in geometric patterns or may spell out a message such as "Greetings from Barbados."

TECHNIQUE

The basic techniques of crafting with shells are quite simple, leaving it very much up to the artisan to create different patterns. Barbadian craftspeople glue shells to boxes, mirrors, and other surfaces. Barbadians drill holes in shells and then string them into necklaces.

Seashells are the hard skeletons of creatures called mollusks. Unlike your skeleton, the shells grow outside the mollusks' bodies. Mollusks include such animals as snails, clams, and scallops. They may live buried in the sand or underwater. When they die, waves may wash their empty shells onto the beach.

Shells and other natural objects decorate woven boxes for sale at a Caribbean souvenir stand.

HOW-TO PROJECT

Decorate a box with shells. You can use a small cardboard box or an inexpensive wooden box from a craft or fabric store. You can collect shells on a beach or buy them from floral suppliers or craft stores.

If you plan to find your own shells, first make sure that shell collecting is allowed at the beach you've chosen. Wash any shells found on a beach in a solution of one gallon of water plus ¼ cup of bleach.

You need:
A small box
1 sheet plain paper
Pencil
Shells
White glue
Toothpicks

1 Draw around the outline of the box on a piece of paper.

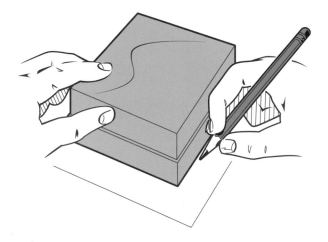

2 Arrange the shells into a pattern within the outline drawn on the paper. It is easy to form a pattern by starting with large shells and filling in empty spaces with smaller shells. Place the shells close together. The more you can fit on the outline, the better your project will look.

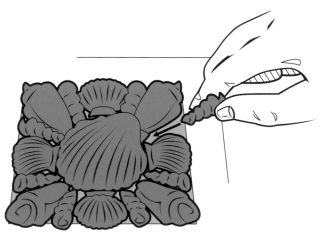

3 Spread some glue on a small area of the box cover. Take shells from your outline and press them on the glue. Press the shells one at a time in the same pattern you arranged on the paper. Use a toothpick to spread more glue over the box and to move shells into place. The glue will dry clear.

WHAT ELSE YOU CAN DO

Other Items: Try decorating other things, such as picture frames or wall plaques. Glue shells to small cardboard or wooden disks to make pendants.

Seeds: Island people use seeds as well as shells for decorations. You can make colorful projects by selecting seeds in various sizes and colors. Did you know that dried beans and peas are seeds? Mix in acorn cups, eucalyptus pods, and other natural materials you find.

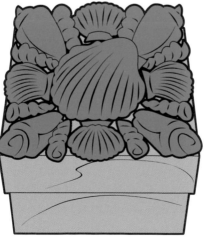

Cuban Yarn Dolls

Yarn dolls are quick, easy, and inexpensive toys.

HOMEMADE TOYS

Making children's toys is an age-old tradition in both the African and Indian cultures that strongly influence Cuban arts and crafts. Cuban children often play with toys that their parents or they themselves make. People might make dolls from yarn, palm leaves, or other materials they find.

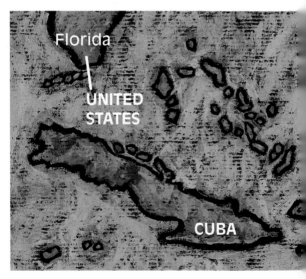

Cuba is the largest island in the Caribbean. European settlers first brought the yarns and fabrics that Cubans use to make dolls.

TECHNIQUE

To make yarn dolls, people wind strands around a piece of cardboard, then tie the bundle together in several places to separate the body, arms, and legs. Craftspeople complete the doll by gluing on seeds, bits of felt, or other materials for the eyes and the mouth.

A Cuban girl cuddles her yarn doll. Her mother or another relative probably made the doll for her.

HOW-TO PROJECT

You need:

A ball or skein of yarn
A piece of cardboard, 8 inches
    by 4 inches
Scissors
Tape
Ribbon (optional)
Small pieces of felt
White glue

1 Tape the end of the ball of yarn to the cardboard. Wind the yarn the long way around the cardboard until there is a bundle about 1 inch thick wrapped around the rectangle. Cut the strand of yarn.

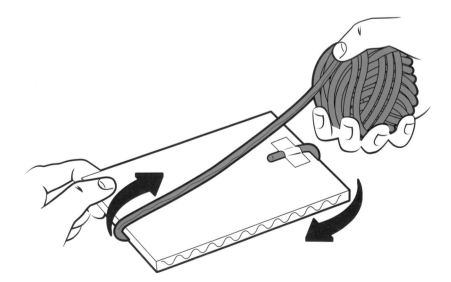

2 Tie the top of the bunch together with a piece of ribbon or yarn. Slide the whole bunch carefully off the cardboard.

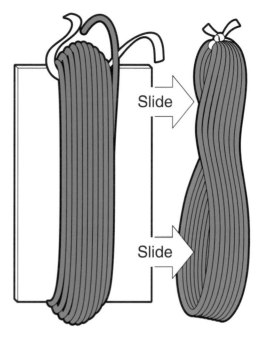

3 About an inch from the top, tie the bundle together to form the head. Cut through the bottom of the bunch of yarn. Your bunch will look like a mop.

4 On one side, grasp a few strands of yarn for an arm. About 2 inches down from the head, wind a piece of yarn or ribbon around the arm several times and knot the strand. Repeat on the other side for the other arm. Trim each arm about ³/₄ inch below the knot.

2 inches

3/4 inch

5 Knot yarn or ribbon around the middle of the doll to create a waist. Divide the loose strands of yarn in two for the legs. About an inch from the bottom, wind yarn or ribbon several times around each leg and knot. Cut the bottom of the legs evenly.

6 Cut eyes, a nose, and a mouth from felt and glue them to the head. Trim the strands of yarn or ribbon you used to tie the doll.

WHAT ELSE YOU CAN DO

Colors: The traditional color for yarn dolls is white, but you can make the dolls any color you want. Make dolls in wild rainbow colors. Use left-over yarn in whatever color you can get.

Clothing and Hair: Dress yarn dolls with fabric scraps. Braid yarn or thread for hair. Dress a whole family with different clothes. Dress a yarn doll in a way that you think a sister, brother, or friend would like. Then give the person the doll as a gift.

Ornaments: Leave long strands of yarn or ribbon on top of the doll's head. Tie these strands into a loop and hang up the doll as a decoration for a birthday, holiday, or other special occasion.

Grenadian Spice Hangers

Spice hangers are made of colorful ribbons and cloth paired with pleasant-smelling spices.

SPICE HANGERS

In the 1800s, when ships approached the island of Grenada (gruh-NAY-duh), sailors could smell nutmeg if the wind was blowing in the right direction. Grenada was called the Spice Island because spices grow especially well in the island's volcanic soil. The crops of nutmeg, mace, cloves, cinnamon, and

GRENADA

South America

Grenada, an island on the southeast end of the Caribbean chain, is about 90 miles north of South America. British colonists first planted nutmeg, Grenada's most important spice, on the island in the early 1840s.

other spices are exported to many countries all over the world and used in local cooking. Grenadian artisans use spices to make souvenirs for tourists. Colorful spice hangers give off a whiff to remind visitors of the Spice Island.

Most of the sweet-smelling spices that grow in the Caribbean are native to Southeast Asia. They include cinnamon, nutmeg, ginger, and cloves. Europeans brought these plants to the Caribbean in the late 1700s and early 1800s. Many Caribbean foods are a mix of Asian spices and native or European ingredients prepared with African, Indian, or European cooking methods.

A Grenadian woman carries a basket of spices that were grown on her island.

HOW-TO PROJECT

Spices for cooking are stored in closed containers. Spices may also be displayed for decoration in spice hangers.

You need:

3 circles of cotton fabric, 5 inches in diameter
Cotton balls
Cooking oil
Spoon
Ground nutmeg
Narrow ribbon, raffia, or yarn
Cardboard, 1½ by 1½ inches
Ribbon, 1½ inches wide and 18 inches long
White glue
Scissors
Hole puncher
Stapler

1 Place two or three cotton balls in the middle of each fabric circle. Dot the cotton with a drop of oil. Carefully spoon on about ½ teaspoon of nutmeg. The oil will keep the nutmeg's aroma alive longer.

2 Gather the fabric around the cotton balls to form a pouch. Knot tightly with ribbon, raffia, or yarn.

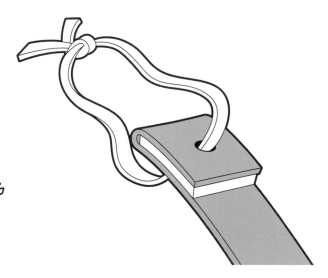

3 Glue the cardboard to the back of the 18-inch ribbon and fold the ribbon over. Trim so the cardboard doesn't show. Allow the glue to dry. Then punch a hole through the reinforced end of the ribbon and tie on a loop for hanging.

4 Space the fabric bundles evenly along the length of ribbon and glue them down. Tie pieces of narrow ribbon, raffia, or yarn into bows and glue or staple them between the bundles.

WHAT ELSE YOU CAN DO

Other Scents: For variety, try different spices, potpourri, cocoa powder, or vanilla and discover which smells you like best.

More Decorations: Glue on seeds, acorns, long curly ribbons, glitter, stickers, colored pompoms, or whatever you like. Tie cinnamon sticks between the spice balls.

Different Hanger: Instead of ribbon, braid several strands of yarn.

Tap-tap Trucks

You can pretend your clay tap-tap truck is taking people home from the market (top). The truck can carry musicians and their drums (middle). Or it can bring a surfer to the beach (bottom).

TAP-TAPS

Brightly colored trucks travel the roads of the Caribbean Islands. The vehicles are called tap-taps, and they take people and belongings wherever the passengers want to go. Many tap-tap trucks are quite old, but their drivers take great care to keep them in good running order. On many islands, tourists can buy comical clay or ceramic model tap-taps. The artists pile the roofs high with

Passengers have climbed right onto the roof of this Haitian tap-tap.

A souvenir shop in Haiti offers a tap-tap truck cutout for sale.

vegetables, fruit, luggage, and household goods, and they sculpt passengers to sit inside or even on the bumper—just like on a real tap-tap.

TECHNIQUE

You can make your own model tap-tap from clay. You will use age-old pottery techniques. The body of the truck is made by joining flat sections of clay. The passengers and cargo are formed by rolling, shaping, and combining pieces of clay.

HOW-TO PROJECT

The tap-tap can be made with any kind of clay. (The project cannot be completed in one day because the clay has to dry before you can paint it.) Self-hardening clay is easiest to use, as it dries in the air. Other types of clay may have to be baked in an oven. Whatever type of clay you use, it is important to follow the directions on the package.

Pieces of clay must always be joined together with water. Dip your fingers in water and moisten the clay on both surfaces to be joined. The water bonds the clay parts together so they will not separate when they dry.

You need:

Sheet of plain paper
Newspaper
Clay
Plastic wrap
Rolling pin or a full bottle with smooth sides
Table knife
Small bowl of water
2 toothpicks, broken in half
Poster or acrylic paints
Paintbrush
White glue

1 Trace or photocopy the pattern on page 33 onto a piece of paper. Cut out the pattern pieces.

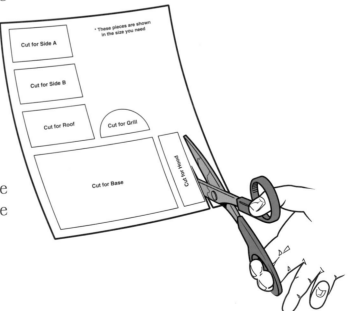

• These pieces are shown in the size you need

Cut for Side A

Cut for Side B

Cut for Roof

Cut for Grill

Cut for Hood

Cut for Base

2 Spread newspapers over your work area. Roll a large lump of clay into a ball. Set it on top of the newspaper and cover it with a piece of plastic wrap. Flatten the clay, first with your hands and then with a rolling pin. You should end up with a slab about ¾ inch thick.

3 Place the truck pattern pieces on top of the clay slab. Cut out the base, roof, sides, hood, and grill with a table knife. Remove the paper.

4 Join the sides to the base. Attach the roof. Bend the rectangle for the hood and attach the grill to one side. Then attach the hood and grill to the front of the truck. Dip your finger in water and smooth all the joints.

5 Fold an extra piece of newspaper in half several times until you have a pad about ½ inch thick and exactly as wide as the base of the tap-tap truck. Set the truck on top of this pad. Roll four ¾-inch balls of clay and flatten them into wheels. Pierce the center of each wheel with a toothpick half. Set each wheel against the base of the truck and push the toothpick into the base.

6 Make people and objects by forming small balls and rolls of clay. Shape them into anything you think may be transported on a tap-tap. When you combine parts, join them with water.

7 Let the truck, the people, and the objects dry completely, which may take a day or two. When the clay is dry, paint it however you like.

8 Glue the passengers and their things to the truck with white glue.

WHAT ELSE YOU CAN DO

Toy Tap-tap: Leave the people and cargo unattached to the truck so you can rearrange the pieces anytime you like. Remember that you must be gentler with clay than with metal or plastic toys, as clay is more breakable.

Repairs: After the clay has dried, parts of the truck may fall off and need to be reattached. You can glue them together with white glue. For tricky joints, you can dip a small piece of a cotton ball in glue and insert it in between the two pieces to be joined. Press the pieces together.

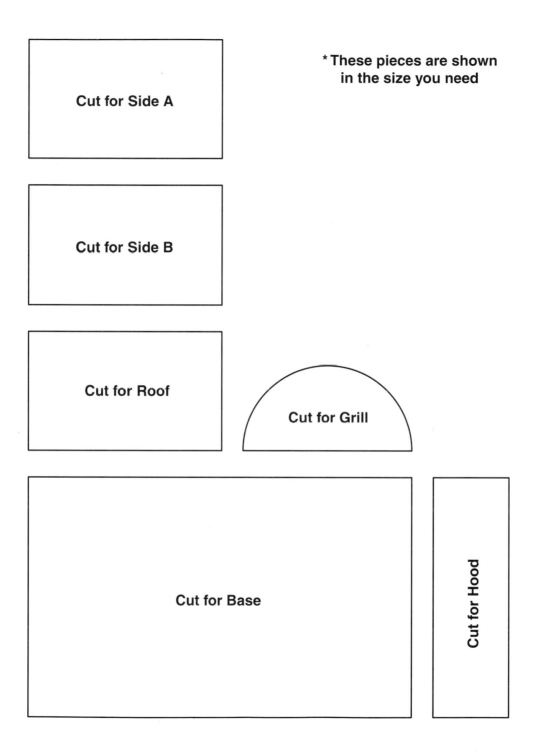

Cut for Side A

* These pieces are shown
in the size you need

Cut for Side B

Cut for Roof

Cut for Grill

Cut for Base

Cut for Hood

Haitian Metal Cutouts

Shiny metal cutouts catch the eye whether hung singly or as a mobile.

FLAT STEEL SCULPTURES

Haitian metal cutouts made from used oil drums began with Georges Liautaud (ZHORZHE lee-oh-TOH), a blacksmith who lived from 1899 to 1992. In the 1950s, as a hobby, Liautaud created sculptures by recycling the steel sheeting from empty oil drums. He became a highly respected artist, and his works inspired others to imitate his methods. Liautaud's type of metal crafting is recognized worldwide as uniquely Haitian.

Haiti is located in the western third of the island of Hispaniola. The Dominican Republic occupies the eastern two-thirds.

TECHNIQUE

To prepare a suitable sheet of metal, Liautaud cut off the top and bottom of an oil drum. Then he cut the barrel open and flattened it into a rectangle measuring 6 feet by 3 feet. Next he scratched on his drawing and cut the outline with heavy shears. He textured the surface by hammering and cutting straight lines and circles into it. Liautaud created mermaids, roosters and other animals, people, supernatural beings, and characters from Haitian folklore.

This metal sculpture hangs in Haiti's National Art Gallery.

Georges Liautaud's style was distinctive. He sometimes used the same form for several of his metal sculptures. Some of his shapes appear below.

HOW-TO PROJECT

You can try this oil drum craft using disposable baking pans sold in supermarkets.

CAUTION: The cut edges of baking tins may be sharp. Work slowly and carefully, and ask an adult to help you. Use old scissors to cut metal, as it will dull the blades.

You need:

Paper and pencil
Old scissors
Disposable aluminum baking pan
Tape
Old newspapers or magazines
Nail, thumbtack, or ballpoint pen
Paper punch

1 Using paper and pencil, draw or trace the outline of one of the patterns on page 39. Or draw your own design. Cut out the outline.

2 Cut off the sides of the baking pan, leaving a flat sheet. Tape the outline to the baking sheet. Carefully cut along the paper outline. Always cut into corners. Remove the paper pattern from your cutout.

3 Cover your work surface with a thick layer of old newspapers or magazines. Lay your cutout face down on the newspapers. Use a nail, thumbtack, or ballpoint pen to press dots or lines into the back of the cutout. Use a paper punch to create large dots. Some marks may go all the way through the metal.

WHAT ELSE YOU CAN DO

Color: Use markers (permanent type is best) or acrylic paints. Authentic Haitian reliefs are dark brown or black, but you can choose any color.

Hanging Decorations: Make small cutouts and hang them as mobiles or holiday ornaments. Punch a hole at the top and loop a piece of yarn or ribbon through it for a hanger.

Greeting Cards: Fold a piece of heavy paper in half. Glue a cutout to the front. Give the card to a friend or mail it in a padded envelope.

Writing: Because you're marking the back of the cutout, you must write words backwards. Trace your cutout right side up on a piece of thin white paper. Write your message on the tracing. Then tape your paper to a window, front side facing out. Trace the writing. Take your pattern from the window, tape your cutout on the outline you drew, and turn the paper over. Trace over the backwards writing with a ballpoint pen, pressing hard so that the lines will appear in the metal.

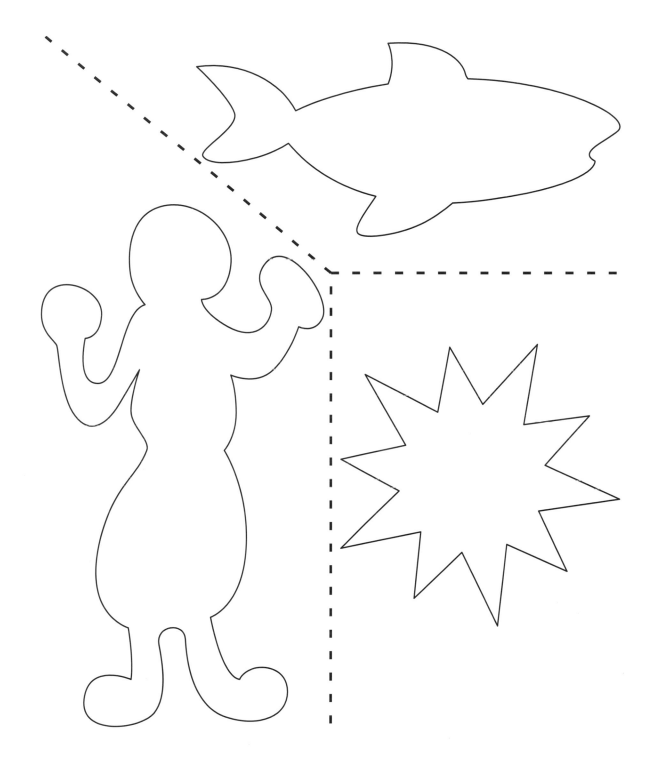

Puerto Rican Vejigante Masks

Historians believe that vejigante masks have their roots in a medieval Spanish festival in which people wore scary costumes to remind each other to go to church.

VEJIGANTE MASKS

At certain festivals in Puerto Rico, masked revelers called *vejigantes* (vay-hee-GAHN-tays) entertain the crowd with their antics. The vejigantes wear polka-dotted clothes and distinctive, fierce masks. The masks have horns, fanglike teeth, and are traditionally painted red, black, and yellow.

Puerto Rico is about 1,000 miles southeast of the U.S. state of Florida. The island's Indian, European, and African ethnic groups all have maskmaking traditions.

40

A Puerto Rican maskmaker presses papier-mâché onto a mold (top right). Modern-day vejigantes dress in traditional clothes (bottom right) or in their own wild color combinations (above).

TECHNIQUE

Puerto Rican maskmakers might construct vejigante masks from wood, coconut husks, gourds, or papier-mâché. Papier-mâché has been used for masks in many parts of the world for centuries because it is strong yet light. Strips of torn paper are glued in layers on the outside of a mold. Caribbean masks are often shaped on plastic molds that can be used over and over again. When the layers are dry, they become a solid form that can be painted and decorated.

HOW-TO PROJECT

You can use an inflated balloon as a mold for making a vejigante mask.

You Need:

Old newspapers
Balloon
Petroleum jelly
Bowl or pot
Library paste, white glue, or wall-
    paper paste
Disposable cup
Cardboard from cereal boxes
Masking tape
A pin
Scissors
A piece of tissue paper
Marker
Poster or acrylic paint
Paintbrush
String

1 Cover your work area with newspaper. Blow up the balloon and close it with a knot. Smear petroleum jelly with your fingers over the front half of the balloon. Set the balloon, smeared side up, on a bowl or pot to keep it from moving while you work on it.

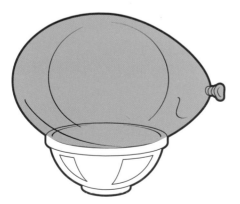

2 Put some paste or glue in a disposable cup. If necessary, dilute it with some water until it flows like heavy cream. Tear newspaper into strips about 4 inches by 1½ inches. Dip a strip into the glue. Run it between two fingers to squeeze out extra glue. Layer the strips in one direction on the balloon, making sure the edges overlap slightly.

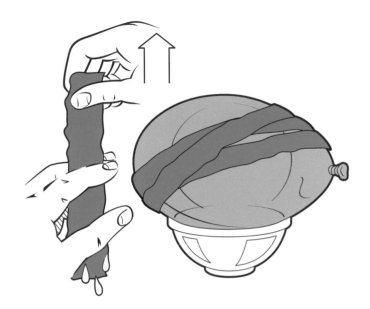

3 Apply three more layers of strips. Each layer should go in the opposite direction of the one beneath. Let the papier-mâché dry completely. Finish the mask with a layer of paste or glue, which will act as a varnish.

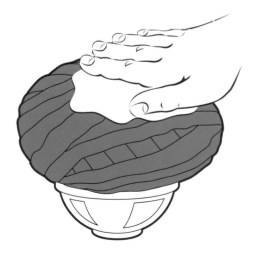

4 Cut two narrow triangles from cardboard for teeth. Cut three cardboard triangles for each horn you wish to add. Stick the long triangles together with masking tape. Cover the teeth and horns with two layers of papier-mâché strips and let them dry.

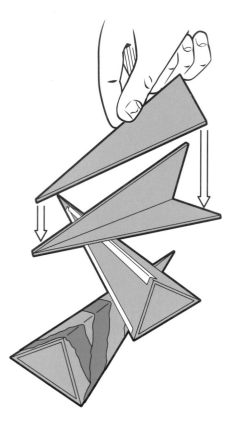

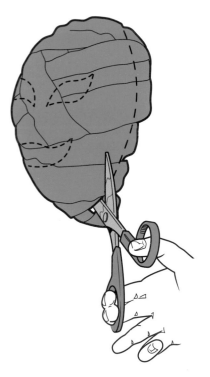

5 When the mask is dry, pierce the balloon with a pin and pull it away. Even out the edges by cutting around with scissors. To cut the mouth and two eyes, place a piece of tissue paper over your face. With a moistened finger, press the paper against your mouth and eyes. Place the paper on top of the mask, mark the three places, and cut the holes. Make a hole on each side of the mask for the strings that hold the mask on your head.

6 Tape the horns and teeth to the mask. Then cover the joints with two layers of papier-mâché strips. Let the mask dry.

7 Paint the mask. To make it look like a traditional vejigante mask, paint specks or dots all over the face and horns. Tie a piece of string to each hole at the side and you're ready to wear your mask.

WHAT ELSE YOU CAN DO

Other Features: Vejigante masks are fierce and bold, so make your mask as colorful and wild as you can. Add feathers, stickers, yarn, large cardboard ears, and anything else you like.

Wall Decorations: Masks are often hung on walls. In that case you don't have to cut out holes for the eyes and mouth. Just paint them on.

Festival Costumes: Make a costume to go with your mask and have a parade with your friends.

Caribbean Drums

It's easy to turn a few household scraps into a new toy drum.

MUSICAL INSTRUMENTS

Caribbean islanders love music for entertainment and dancing. African people brought a tradition of drumming to the islands. That tradition influenced the development of calypso (cuh-LIHP-soh), reggae (REHG-gay), merengue (may-RAYN-gay), salsa, and many other musical rhythmic styles. Musicians often produce rhythms on percussion instruments, which are played by striking them with the hands or with sticks. Caribbean musicians play many kinds of drums made of wood or metal.

TECHNIQUE

Caribbean instruments vary a great deal in their design because islanders make their instruments from natural materials, such as gourds, reeds, coconuts, and other things that they find. But all instruments have some things in common. A musical instrument produces sounds when a player vibrates some part of it. The vibrations create waves in the air, and our ears perceive these waves as sound. Most instruments have hollow spaces that amplify the sounds.

Caribbean musicians play their drums for fun or to earn money from passers-by.

HOW-TO PROJECT

You can create the rhythmic beat of the Caribbean by making a very simple drum out of a coffee can. Cans of different sizes will produce different sounds. Do not use any cans that have rough edges, as these could cut you while you work on them.

You need:

Empty coffee can and lid, washed, any label removed
Self-adhesive shelf liner printed with a wood-grain design
White glue
8-inch circle of white cotton muslin
String or twine
Dowels or chopsticks (optional)

1 Use a piece of string to measure the height and distance around your coffee can. Cut a piece of shelf liner to fit your can, adding half an inch to the width. Make sure the wood grain runs parallel to the short side of the rectangle.

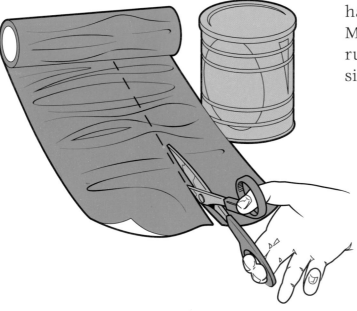

2 Peel an inch of the backing off the shelf liner to leave a short length of adhesive exposed. Fit the liner onto the can. Lay the drum, liner side down, onto a flat surface. Peel the backing off the liner with one hand and roll the drum onto the liner with the other hand.

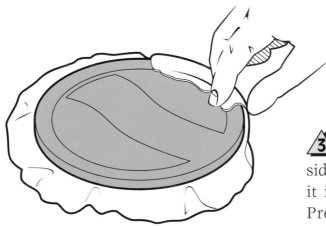

3 Spread glue on the top and sides of the coffee can lid and place it in the center of the fabric circle. Press down. Fold the edges of the fabric over the rim of the lid and place the lid on the open end of the coffee can.

4 Real Caribbean drums have tuning strings—a system of cords that holds the cover onto the drum and that can change the instrument's sound. To show tuning strings on your drum, glue a piece of string or twine around the middle of the drum. Cut shorter pieces of twine to glue around the outside of the drum in the pattern shown.

5 Drums can be beaten with your hands or with sticks. Use dowels or chopsticks.

WHAT ELSE YOU CAN DO

Sections: Instead of using a solid piece of shelf liner, use strips of dark and light material to make your drum look like it is made of different kinds of wood.

Different Paper: You can use a brown paper shopping bag instead of shelf liner. Tape one end of the paper to the coffee can. Wrap the paper around the can and tape or glue the ends of the paper together where they overlap.

Another Drumstick: Soften the sound of your drum by wrapping the ends of your drumsticks with cloth or masking tape.

Carrying Cord: Measure out a piece of cord long enough to loop over your head and one shoulder and hang at your waist. Add 2 feet to the length and cut the cord. Tie the cord around your drum and then knot the two ends.

Rhythm Band: Make many instruments in different sizes. Compare the sounds they produce. Practice playing the instruments with your friends.

Jamaican Woven Fish

Plain or fancy woven fish can decorate a greeting card, a school report, party invitations, or whatever else you can imagine.

PALM WEAVING

In Jamaica children often pick up a palm frond (leaf) and weave it into a bird, a rose, a fish, or any number of other things. They continue a long island tradition of weaving strips of coconut palm fronds into mats, hats, containers, brooms, toys, and decorations. Families make them for their own use or for sale in street markets where stalls are set up in rows. Some stands are even screened overhead with palm fronds to reflect the hot sun.

CUBA

JAMAICA

Jamaica is about 90 miles south of Cuba and 110 miles west of Haiti. Islanders have been weaving palm leaves and other natural materials since the days of Jamaica's earliest inhabitants.

A Jamaican weaver carries fresh palm fronds under his arm. Fronds grow as separate leaflets on a central rib. Depending on whether fronds are intended for a basket, a mat, or something else, weavers may leave the leaflets attached to the rib or pull them off to use separately.

TECHNIQUE

Weavers collect fresh palm fronds and let them dry for a few days. This prevents a finished weaving from developing holes later on because the strips have shrunk.

For flat mats, horizontal strips, called the weft, are woven over and under vertical strips, called the warp. Once weavers understand this basic method, they like to make their work more interesting by varying patterns. They may weave two strips over and two under or try any of many other possible combinations.

HOW-TO PROJECT

Weave a fish by interlacing paper strips instead of palm leaves. For your first try, it is easier to use vertical strips in one color and horizontal strips in another color. If you live in an area where palms grow, you can weave with fronds that have fallen on the ground.

You need:

2 pieces of paper, 8 inches long
   by 2 inches wide
Scissors
Glue
Toothpick
Pen

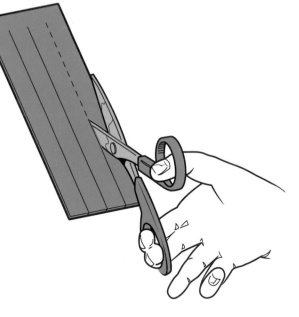

1 On one piece of paper, cut long slits about 1/2 inch apart, but do not cut all the way to top.

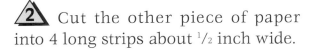

2 Cut the other piece of paper into 4 long strips about ¹/₂ inch wide.

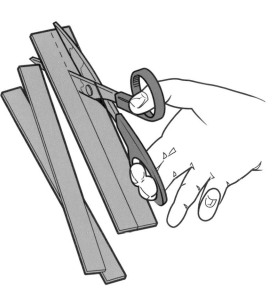

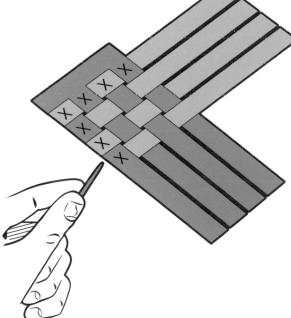

3 Weave the loose strips over and under, as shown. Push them close together. Glue the weaving together where you see the crosses, in between the two layers of paper. Dipping a toothpick into glue helps.

4 Cut off the solid pieces at the top and side.

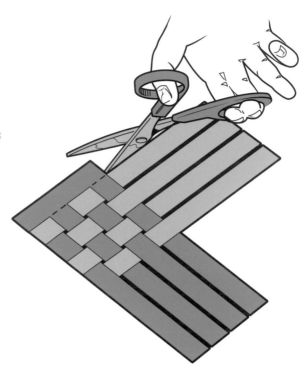

5 Place the weaving sideways. To shape the fins, draw lines at an angle beginning at the corners of the weaving, as shown. Cut on the lines. Draw on an eye.

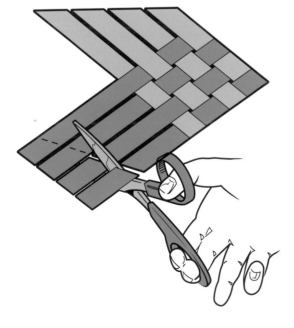

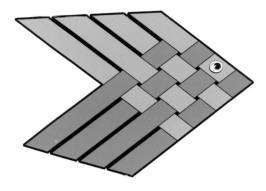

WHAT ELSE YOU CAN DO

Decorating: You can glue confetti or sequins on the fish.

Trim the Fins: Cut the ends into curves or feathery fins. Fold or cut off some of the middle fin strips to change the look of your fish.

Whirling Toy: In Jamaica, children sometimes attach woven fish to a long palm rib to make a toy they can swing or whirl. Tie a 12-inch piece of thread to the mouth of the fish. Tie the other end of the thread to a stick.

Mobile: Make several woven fish. Tape thread to the top of each fish. Then tape or tie the other end of the thread to a coat hanger, a dowel, or around the rim of a paper plate. Tape or tie another piece of thread to the center of your plate or dowel. Your mobile is ready to hang up.

Different Sizes: Weave the fish with bigger pieces of paper and wider strips. Make them big enough for a placemat or a greeting card. Or try smaller pieces of paper and narrower strips. Make kitchen magnets or glue the fish to drawings or school reports.

METRIC CONVERSION CHART

If you want to use the metric system, convert measurements using the chart on the right. Because fractions can be hard to work with, round all metric measurements to the nearest whole number.

when you know:	multiply by:	to find:
Length		
inches	25.00	millimeters
inches	2.54	centimeters
feet	30.00	centimeters
feet	.30	meters
yards	.91	meters
miles	1.61	kilometers
Volume		
teaspoons	5.00	milliliters
tablespoons	15.00	milliliters
fluid ounces	30.00	milliliters
cups	0.24	liters
pints	0.47	liters
quarts	0.95	liters
gallons	3.80	liters
Weight		
ounces	28.00	grams
pounds	0.45	kilograms

GLOSSARY

artisan: A person who is very skilled at making crafts

ceramic: Made of baked clay

culture: The customs, ideas, and traditions of a certain group of people. Culture includes religious celebrations, arts and crafts, folktales, costumes, and food.

frond: A long leaf that divides into many parts

medieval: Relating to a period of European history that lasted from about A.D. 500 to 1500.

mobile: A sculpture made of hanging parts that can turn in the breeze

oil drum: A metal barrel for holding fuel oil, usually 55 gallons

papier-mâché: Torn or shredded paper mixed with glue

percussion instrument: A musical instrument that is played by hitting or shaking

raffia: The dried fiber of the raffia palm tree leaf

rhythm: A pattern of beats, such as in music or poetry

Southeast Asia: A geographical region that includes the nations of Myanmar, Thailand, Laos, Cambodia, Vietnam, Malaysia, the Philippines, Singapore, Brunei, and Indonesia

souvenir: An object that people keep to remind them of an event such as a vacation

tropical: A zone around the middle of the earth where the weather is hot and wet

warp: The vertical (up and down) fibers in a piece of weaving

weft: The horizontal (across) fibers in a piece of weaving. The weft fills in the spaces created by the warp.

READ MORE ABOUT THE CARIBBEAN

Fiction & Folktales

Agard, John, and Grace Nichols, editors. *A Caribbean Dozen: Poems from Caribbean Poets.* Illustrations by Cathie Felstead. Cambridge, Mass.: Candlewick Press, 1994.

Gershator, Phillis. *Rata-pata-scata-fata: A Caribbean Story.* Illustrations by Holly Meade. Boston: Little, Brown, 1994.

Hanson, Regina. *The Tangerine Tree.* Illustrations by Harvey Stevenson. New York: Clarion, 1995.

Lessac, Frané. *Caribbean Alphabet.* Illustrations by the author. New York: Tambourine Books, 1989.

Lessac, Frané (illustrator). *Caribbean Canvas.* New York: J.B. Lippincott, 1989.

Orr, Katherine. *My Grandpa and the Sea.* Illustrations by the author. Minneapolis: Carolrhoda, 1990.

Orr, Katherine. *Story of a Dolphin.* Illustrations by the author. Minneapolis: Carolrhoda, 1993.

Pomerantz, Charlotte. *The Chalk Doll.* Illustrations by Frané Lessac. New York: J.B. Lippincott, 1989.

Williams, Karen Lynn. *Tap Tap.* Illustrations by Catherine Stock. New York: Clarion, 1994.

Nonfiction

Broberg, Merle. *Barbados*. Philadelphia: Chelsea House Publishers, 1999.

Capek, Michael. *Jamaica* (Globetrotters Club). Minneapolis: Carolrhoda Books, Inc., 1999.

Hintz, Martin. *Haiti* (Enchantment of the World). Danbury, CT: Children's Press, 1998.

Johnston, Joyce. *Puerto Rico* (Hello USA). Minneapolis: Lerner Publications Company, 1994.

Kaufman, Cheryl. *Cooking the Caribbean Way*. Minneapolis: Lerner Publications Company, 1988.

Milivojevic, JoAnn. *Puerto Rico* (Globetrotters Club). Carolrhoda Books, Inc., 2000.

Staub, Frank. *Children of Cuba*. Minneapolis: Carolrhoda Books, Inc., 1998.

Urosevich, Patricia R. *Trinidad and Tobago*. Philadelphia: Chelsea House Publishers, 1999.

INDEX

ABOUT THE AUTHOR

Florence Temko is an internationally known author of more than 40 books on world folk crafts and paper arts. She has traveled in 31 countries, gaining much of her skill firsthand. Ms. Temko shows her enthusiasm for crafts through simple, inventive adaptations of traditional arts and crafts projects. She has presented hundreds of hands-on programs in schools and museums, including the Metropolitan Museum of Art in New York City and the Children's Museum in Boston. She lives in San Diego, California, where she is a consultant for the Mingei International Museum.

ACKNOWLEDGMENTS

The photographs in this book are reproduced with the permission of:

Turkish Republic, Ministry of Culture and Tourism, p. 6 (left); Wilford Archaeology Laboratory, University of Minnesota, by Kathy Raskob/IPS, p. 6 (right); Nelson-Atkins Museum of Art, Kansas City, Missouri (Purchase: Nelson Trust), p. 7 (left); Freer Gallery of Art, Smithsonian Institution, p. 7 (right); Robert L. and Diane Wolfe, pp. 8, 9; IPS, pp. 12, 16, 22, 26, 24, 40, 46, 52; Corbis: (© Wolfgang Kaehler) pp. 13 , 23, (© Mike Zens) p. 53; Jimmy Dorantes/Latin Focus.com, p. 17; © Sean Sprague/Panos Pictures, p. 27 (left); © Len Kaufman, p. 27 (right); © Maxine Cass, p. 35; © Suzanne Murphy-Larronde/DDB Stock Photography, p. 41 (all); © TRIP/J. Greenberg, p. 47.

Front cover photograph by IPS.

The maps on pages 11, 12, 22, 24, 34, and 52 are by John Erste. The illustrations on pages 2, 11, 13, 23, and 35 are by Laura Westlund.